W9-BRI-948

THE Big Island

IMAGES OF HAWAI'I ISLAND

Photography by

Douglas Peebles

Mutual Publishing

Library of Congress Catalog Card Number: 2004106191

ISBN 1-56647-671-2

First Printing, July 2004
Second Printing, July 2005
2 3 4 5 6 7 8 9

Mutual Publishing, LLC
1215 Center Street, Suite 210
Honolulu, Hawai'i 96816
Ph: (808) 732-1709 / Fax: (808) 734-4094
e-mail: mutual@mutualpublishing.com
www.mutualpublishing.com
Printed in Taiwan

A vibrant sunset casts orange and red hues atop Kīlauea Volcano.

Once rich in native vegetation, the slopes of Hāmākua Coast today are cast mostly with foreign plants and trees that have been introduced to the area.

The placid, deep blue waters of Reed's Bay in Hilo have become a popular boating harbor.

The slopes of Mauna Kea rise behind the pastures of Parker Ranch.

Waterfalls cascade down the North Kohala Coast from Waipi'o to Pololū Valley.

Kiʻi images such as those found at the Puʻuhonua National Park represented god figures during ancient Hawaiian times.

Lehua blossoms from the ʻōhia tree offer rare bursts of color amidst
the monochromatic landscape of lava rock.

Ferns grow on Kīlauea Iki, a small crater just outside of
Kīlauea Crater at the Hawai'i Volcanoes National Park.

A stunning sunset at Kohala is framed between coconut palms.

The Hawaiian name for Rainbow Falls, Waiānuenue, means "water of the rainbow."

These coffee cherries, almost completely ripe, are grown at the Uchida coffee farm.

Mauna Kea Observatory is the perfect place from
which to view the heavens.

The Big Island's three tallest peaks, Hualālai with Mauna Kea and Mauna Loa in the background, peek through a blanket of clouds.

Pu'uhonua, where the City of Refuge National Historical Park is located, fittingly means "a place of refuge."

St. Benedict's Catholic Church is known as
"The Painted Church of Hōnaunau."

The countryside of Waimea offers idyllic charm.

A taro grower holds up a championship sample of taro, or kalo, in Waipiʻo Valley.

Snow-capped Mauna Kea oversees the shores
of Kauna'oa Beach.

Anthuriums are plentiful and colorful on the Big Island.

The fertile land of Waipiʻo Valley is ideal for growing kalo, or taro fields.

The presence of a lush rainforest provides strong contrast to the usual
Big Island images of fire and lava.

Kīlauea Volcano erupts a lava stream, which will
eventually flow into the ocean.

A Hawaiian sunset is always magnificent with swirling colors.

Black sand beaches, such as Keawaiki Bay in Kona, is formed by the residual lava washed ashore from the ocean after a volcanic eruption.

Traditional taro fields thrive in the isolated valleys of the Big Island.

The Big Island is known for its plummeting waterfalls and breathtaking vistas.

Hula is celebrated throughout Hawai'i, especially during the Merrie Monarch Festival, which takes place in Hilo every year.

This hale, or grass hut, stands on the grounds of the Moʻokini Heiau—
a sacred burial ground—in Kohala.

The petroglyphs, or Hawaiian carvings, at Puakō are on one of the
largest petroglyph fields in the islands.

'Anaeho'omalu Bay is one of the most exquisite beaches on the Kohala Coast.

A black lava anchialine pond in Kaʻūpūlehu recreates the ancient fish ponds of the aliʻi, or royalty, of old Hawaiʻi.

The classic Cattleya orchid can be seen in nurseries and gardens on the Big Island.

On a typical day, a cruise ship sits off shore surrounded by small pleasure craft by the Kailua-Kona coastline. PHOTO BY KIRK LEE AEDER

A hawksbill turtle—a rare and endangered species—rests on the black sand at Punaluʻu Beach.

A distant view of Mt. Hualālai exudes a stately solitude and serenity in the early morning.

Hāpuna Beach is one of the few white sand beaches on the Big Island.

Kīlauea Volcano explodes with fiery, red lava.

Kaʻūpūlehu in North Kona is a place tied to different legends about Pele and Mt. Hualālai.

An eruption from Kīlauea Volcano spills into the sea and shatters the surf.